INCREDIBLE
ANIMAL
FACE-OFFS

★ ANIMAL ★

PREDATOR SMACKDOWN

ELSIE OLSON

Consulting Editor, Diane Craig, M.A./Reading Specialist

Super Sandcastle

An Imprint of Abdo Publishing
abdobooks.com

abdobooks.com

Published by Abdo Publishing, a division of ABDO, PO Box 398166, Minneapolis, Minnesota 55439. Copyright © 2020 by Abdo Consulting Group, Inc. International copyrights reserved in all countries. No part of this book may be reproduced in any form without written permission from the publisher. Super Sandcastle™ is a trademark and logo of Abdo Publishing.

Printed in the United States of America, North Mankato, Minnesota
102019
012020

THIS BOOK CONTAINS
RECYCLED MATERIALS

Design: Sarah DeYoung, Mighty Media, Inc.
Production: Mighty Media, Inc.
Editor: Jessica Rusick
Cover Photographs: Shutterstock Images
Interior Photographs: Getty Images/iStockphoto, p. 22; Shutterstock Images, pp. 4, 5, 6, 7, 8, 9, 10, 11, 12, 13, 14, 15, 16, 17, 18, 19, 20, 21, 22 (inset), 23

Library of Congress Control Number: 2019943347

Publisher's Cataloging-in-Publication Data
Names: Olson, Elsie, author.
Title: Animal predator smackdown / by Elsie Olson
Description: Minneapolis, Minnesota : Abdo Publishing, 2020 | Series: Incredible animal face-offs
Identifiers: ISBN 9781532191961 (lib. bdg.) | ISBN 9781532178764 (ebook)
Subjects: LCSH: Predatory animals--Behavior--Juvenile literature. | Display behavior in animals--Juvenile
    literature. | Aggression in animals--Juvenile literature. | Animals, Habits and behavior of--Juvenile
    literature. | Social behavior in animals--Juvenile literature. | Feeding behavior in animals--Juvenile
    literature.
Classification: DDC 591.53--dc23

Super Sandcastle™ books are created by a team of professional educators, reading specialists, and content developers around five essential components—phonemic awareness, phonics, vocabulary, text comprehension, and fluency—to assist young readers as they develop reading skills and strategies and increase their general knowledge. All books are written, reviewed, and leveled for guided reading, early reading intervention, and Accelerated Reader™ programs for use in shared, guided, and independent reading and writing activities to support a balanced approach to literacy instruction.

CONTENTS

Battle of the Predators   4

Teamwork Takedown   6

Stealth Showdown   12

Fearsome Flier Battle   18

Glossary   24

BATTLE OF THE PREDATORS

ORCA

The animal kingdom is full of stars. But some animals stand out. These animals are the deadliest predators.

Predators survive by eating other animals. They must catch and kill their prey.

Animal hunters are all around us. But what if you matched them up in face-offs? Which animal would be the toughest predator?

KOMODO DRAGON

DRAGONFLY

GOLDEN
EAGLE

JAGUAR

LIONESS

5

TEAMWORK TAKEDOWN

Orca whales are powerful predators. Lions are too! But which animal would win a teamwork takedown?

Large brains and high intelligence

ORCA
SEA ASSASSIN

This deadly **mammal** hunts great white sharks. Get on your feet for the astounding orca!

Teeth up to 4 inches (10 cm) long tear prey apart

Black-and-white coloring makes whales harder for prey to spot

Communicates using whistles, clicks, and pops

ORCA STATS

HOME
Oceans around the world

FOOD
Fish, marine **mammals**, seabirds, penguins, shark livers, and squid

SIZE
Up to 32 feet (10 m) long and 6 tons (5.4 t)

AN ORCA IS LARGER THAN A PICKUP TRUCK.

PICKUP TRUCK

ORCA

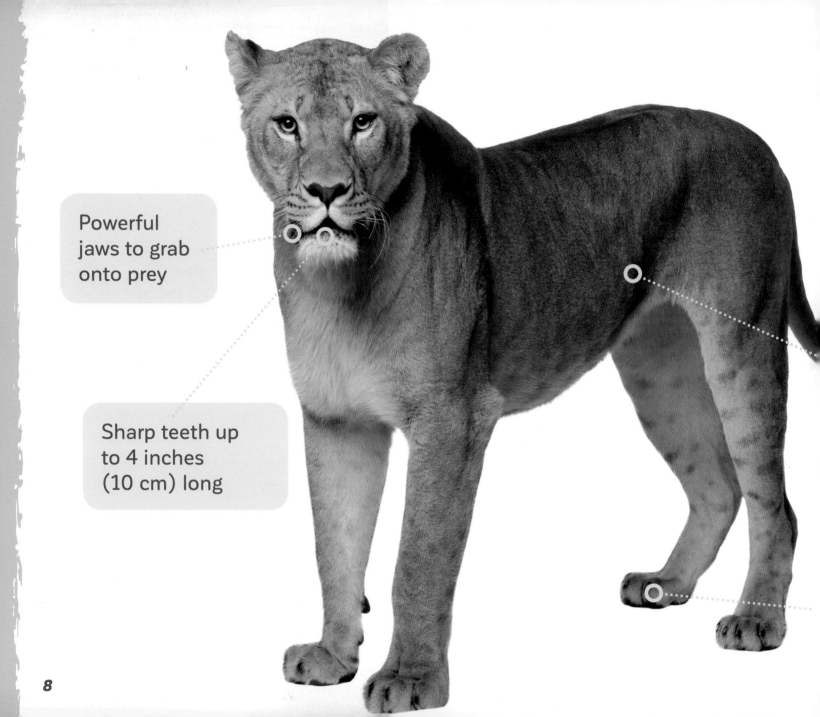

Powerful jaws to grab onto prey

Sharp teeth up to 4 inches (10 cm) long

8

LIONESS
LETHAL LADY

This big cat rules the African **savanna**. Get to know the powerful lioness!

Light brown coloring to blend in with surroundings

Sharp, **retractable** claws up to 1½ inches (4 cm) long

LIONESS STATS

HOME
Deserts and grasslands in Africa and Gir Forest in India

FOOD
Large **mammals**, including zebras, giraffes, and wildebeest

SIZE
Up to 5 feet (1.5 m) long and 400 pounds (181 kg)

A LIONESS IS SHORTER THAN A TWIN BED.

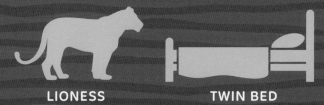

LIONESS   TWIN BED

TEAMWORK TAKEDOWN

ORCA VS LIONESS

ORCA

Orcas hunt in groups called pods. Orcas communicate in clicks and whistles. This helps them catch prey as a team.

HOW THEY HUNT

Orcas hunt in different ways. They make waves near seals. This knocks seals off ice. And they slap sharks with their tails. This flips sharks upside down.

THAT'S TEAMWORK!

A pod can have up to 40 orcas.

LIONESS

Lions live in groups called prides. Female lions are called lionesses. They do most of the pride's hunting.

HOW THEY HUNT

A group of lionesses will slowly circle prey. Then one lioness will chase the prey toward her group.

THAT'S TEAMWORK!

Lionesses usually hunt in groups of two to four.

STEALTH SHOWDOWN

Sharp, strong teeth for tearing into prey

Jaguars are masters of **ambush** hunting. Komodo dragons are too! But which animal would win a stealth showdown?

Curved, **retractable** claws to hold onto prey

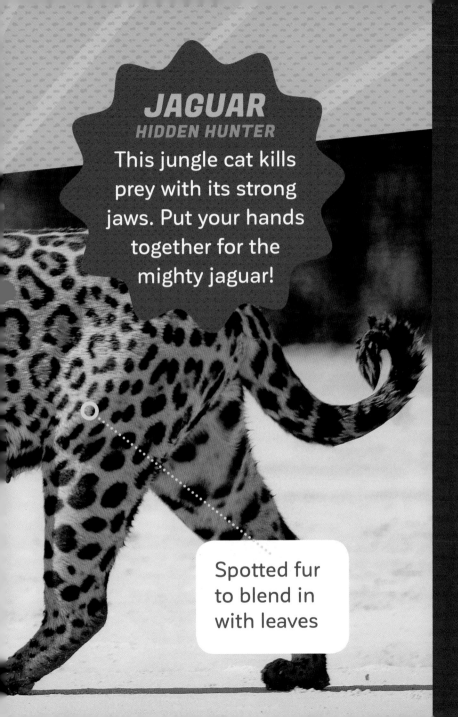

JAGUAR
HIDDEN HUNTER

This jungle cat kills prey with its strong jaws. Put your hands together for the mighty jaguar!

Spotted fur to blend in with leaves

JAGUAR STATS

HOME
Forests, deserts, and mountains in Mexico, Central America, and South America

FOOD
Reptiles, **mammals**, fish, and birds

SIZE
Up to 6 feet (2 m) long and 250 pounds (113 kg)

A JAGUAR IS SHORTER THAN A CANOE.

JAGUAR

CANOE

60 sharp teeth to bite prey

Long tongue to smell prey

KOMODO DRAGON
PATIENT PREDATOR

This large lizard has a mouth full of poison. Make some noise for the Komodo dragon!

Dull scales to blend in with surroundings

Sharp claws

KOMODO DRAGON STATS

HOME
Forests and grasslands on five Indonesian islands

FOOD
Almost any animal, including snakes, deer, and water buffalo

SIZE
Up to 10 feet (3 m) long and more than 300 pounds (136 kg)

A KOMODO DRAGON IS SMALLER THAN A CAR.

KOMODO DRAGON   CAR

JAGUAR VS KOMODO DRAGON

JAGUAR

Jaguars live and hunt alone. They can kill prey with one swipe of a paw. And their jaws can crack a turtle shell!

HOW THEY HUNT

Jaguars sneak up on prey. The big cats also hide in trees. They wait to **pounce** on prey below.

THAT'S SNEAKY!

Jaguars are great swimmers. They can even sneak up on prey in the water.

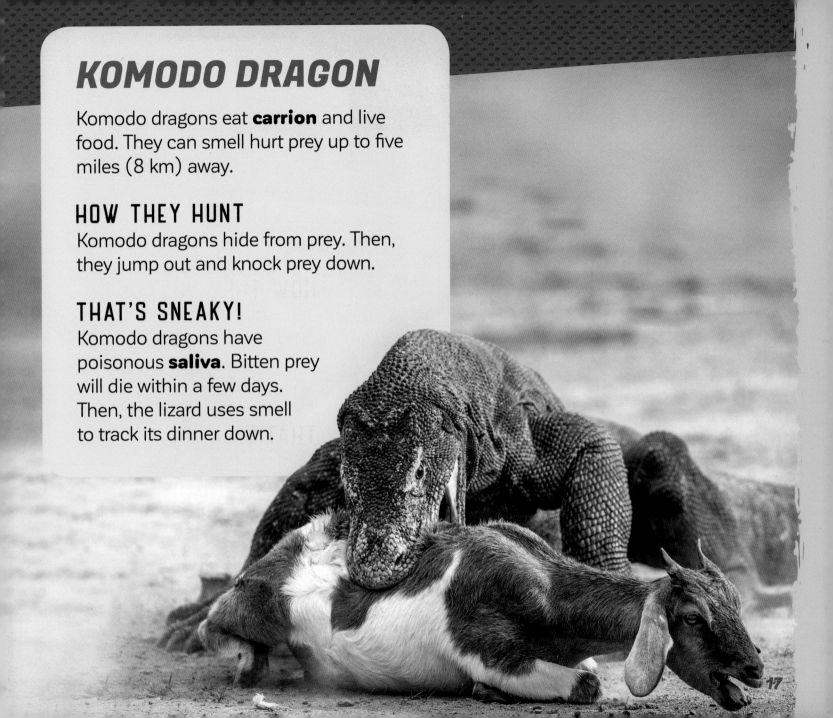

KOMODO DRAGON

Komodo dragons eat **carrion** and live food. They can smell hurt prey up to five miles (8 km) away.

HOW THEY HUNT
Komodo dragons hide from prey. Then, they jump out and knock prey down.

THAT'S SNEAKY!
Komodo dragons have poisonous **saliva**. Bitten prey will die within a few days. Then, the lizard uses smell to track its dinner down.

17

FEARSOME FLIER BATTLE

Long, slim body

Dragonflies are deadly winged predators. Golden eagles are too! But which animal would win a fearsome flier battle?

Two pairs of wings can beat together or separately

Powerful jaws to snatch prey

DRAGONFLY
TIGER OF THE SKY

This insect is one of the best hunters on Earth. Say hello to the deadly dragonfly!

Giant eyes for almost 360-degree vision

Tiny spines on legs to hold onto prey

DRAGONFLY STATS

HOME
Near fresh water all over the world

FOOD
Small insects, including flies, bees, and mosquitoes

SIZE
Up to 5 inches (13 cm) long

A DRAGONFLY IS SHORTER THAN A PENCIL.

DRAGONFLY   PENCIL

Hooked beak to tear into prey

Excellent eyesight

Sharp **talons** to snatch prey

Powerful wings

GOLDEN EAGLE
DEADLY DIVER

This bird can dive at speeds faster than most racecars drive. Give it up for the outstanding golden eagle!

GOLDEN EAGLE STATS

HOME
Mountains, canyons, and forests in North America, Asia, Europe and parts of Africa

FOOD
Small **mammals**, reptiles, fish, and other birds

SIZE
Up to 15 pounds (7 kg) with a 7½-foot (2.3 m) wingspan

A GOLDEN EAGLE'S WINGSPAN IS WIDER THAN AN AVERAGE MAN IS TALL.

GOLDEN EAGLE   MAN

DRAGONFLY VS GOLDEN EAGLE

DRAGONFLY

Dragonflies can see in slow motion. This helps them track speedy prey.

HOW THEY HUNT

A dragonfly snatches an insect with its legs. Then it crushes the insect with its jaws.

THAT'S FAST!

Dragonflies can fly up to 30 miles per hour (48 kmh). They can fly in any direction. They can even hover like helicopters!

GOLDEN EAGLE

Golden eagles often hunt in groups of two. They can spot prey more than one mile (1.6 km) away.

HOW THEY HUNT

Golden eagles usually swoop down on prey. They snatch and kill the prey with their **talons**. Then they use their beaks to eat.

THAT'S FAST!

A golden eagle can fly up to 30 miles per hour (48 kmh). It can dive at almost 150 miles per hour (241 kmh)!

GLOSSARY

ambush—a surprise attack from a hidden position.

carrion—flesh of dead animals.

mammal—a warm-blooded animal that has hair and whose females produce milk to feed their young.

pounce—to jump suddenly on something in order to catch it.

retractable—able to be pulled back in.

saliva—a liquid produced in the mouth.

savanna—a grassland with few trees.

talon—the claw of an animal, especially that of a bird of prey.